How to Grow Marijuana

The Essential Beginner's Guide for Big Buds

How to Grow Marijuana

Copyright 2016 by Tom Whistler - All rights reserved.

This document is geared towards providing exact and reliable information in regards to the topic and issue covered. The publication is sold with the idea that the publisher is not required to render accounting, officially permitted, or otherwise, qualified services. If advice is necessary, legal or professional, a practiced individual in the profession should be ordered.

From a Declaration of Principles which was accepted and approved equally by a Committee of the American Bar Association and a Committee of Publishers and Associations.

In no way is it legal to reproduce, duplicate, or transmit any part of this document in either electronic means or in printed format. Recording of this publication is strictly prohibited and any storage of this document is not allowed unless with written permission from the publisher. All rights reserved.

The information provided herein is stated to be truthful and consistent, in that any liability, in terms of inattention or otherwise, by any usage or abuse of any policies, processes, or directions contained within is the solitary and utter responsibility of the recipient reader. Under no circumstances will any legal responsibility or blame be held against the publisher for any reparation, damages, or monetary loss due to the information herein, either directly or indirectly.

Respective authors own all copyrights not held by the publisher.

The information herein is offered for informational purposes solely, and is universal as so. The presentation of the information is without contract or any type of guarantee assurance.

The trademarks that are used are without any consent, and the publication of the trademark is without permission or backing by the trademark owner. All trademarks and brands within this book are for clarifying purposes only and are the owned by the owners themselves, not affiliated with this document.

Table of Contents

Introduction 4

Chapter One-The Basics..5

Chapter Two-The Tent 8

Chapter Three-Vegetative Growth 12

Chapter Four- Flowering 15

Chapter Five-Harvest 17

Chapter Six-Drying 19

Chapter Seven-Recap and Suggestions...21

Conclusion..23

Introduction

I want to thank you and congratulate you for downloading the book, "How to grow Marijuana: The Essential Beginner's Guide for Big Buds".

This book contains proven steps and strategies on how to grow Marijuana efficiently.

Make sure to follow the steps provided in this book as it is written in a step by step format. If you follow the steps listen in this book without deviating you should be well on your way to growing your own marijuana!

Thanks again for downloading this book, I hope you enjoy it!

Chapter One-The Basics

First, let's start off with a statement. Growing marijuana is no simple task. One cannot go to a dispensary, purchase a plant and expect it to grow premium buds. There is a little bit of work involved, but we'll go over the basics, which will make your first grow an easy and possibly even fun experience. What we will cover in this beginner's guide is the simplest way to grow great buds without delving into all the different avenues. To start off, the most elementary way to get into growing is to purchase clones, not seeds. We'll discuss clones, repotting as they grow, light sources, nutrients and water.

An important thing to remember is, cannabis *is* a plant. In order to have a successful crop, the grower needs to have adequate light, dry air, clean water, nutrients, heat and a previously chosen place to grow. This could be an entire room or basement. If space is an issue, there is also the option to purchase a grow box or tent, either of which can be small enough to fit in the back of a closet or, larger tents can take up an entire corner of a bedroom.

Once you've decided where to grow your plants and what medium to use, the next step is to purchase the necessary items for a successful crop. Remember that the upfront expense might seem daunting, but the outcome will make it all worthwhile. After you've successfully grown a crop or two, there will be no more need to purchase marijuana, saving more money in the long run.

The success of an indoor grower depends heavily on their determination, patience and quality of items used to grow your crop. Below, you will find the items you need in brief detail. Keep in mind that these are the bare minimum. After you've found what works best, you'll be able to expand and try new ways to grow your crop.

Light. Regardless of whether you use a tent, box or are able to dedicate an entire room to your crop, light is a huge component of healthy plants. At various points throughout the process, plants will be under lights for twelve to sixteen hours per day. The two most popular lights are HID and LED. HID has been the most used as LED is new to the indoor growing game. The HID lights require two separate kinds. The Metal Halide, which is used in the vegetative state and the High Pressure Sodium light used mostly during the flowering stage. However, the HPS light can be used throughout the entire process.

Even though the LED technology is new, it is a wonderful alternative. The people who've used it and written reviews or discussed it in forums are loving the LED lights. They are referred to as full-spectrum LED because they can be used the entire lifecycle of the plant. The LED light is costlier but in the long run, you'll save more on your energy bill. Another great selling point of the LED light is it produces less heat than the HID. Either way, you'll need a good ventilation system, though if you used LED, the ventilation wouldn't need to be as intense.

Water and nutrients are also key components to growing big, healthy plants. You might be thinking that dumping water straight from the tap is okay. After all, they are just plants, right? Wrong. In order to grow healthy plants with premium buds, your water needs the right balance of calcium and magnesium. If the water is too "hard" or "soft", it can seriously damage or even kill your plants. Optimum water will have between 100 and 150mg of calcium per liter. In addition to calcium, make sure to check the pH balance. This can be done with relatively inexpensive pH test strips purchased from Walmart or any online outlet. The strip packages detail what good levels of pH are in your water.

Like humans, cannabis plants also require food. The great thing about food for your plants is, it usually comes in pre-mixed solutions. If you've decided to use a high quality soil, you won't need to worry about nutrients or "food" for the first four weeks. The first stage of your grow is called the vegetative state. This is where the plants really take hold and, if properly cared for, will grow strong roots and eventually produce big buds. As previously stated, it is highly recommended you purchase quality items for your crop. The same ideal applies to soil. Rich soil will already be high in nutrients, which will save you some time and effort in being able to forgo feeding your plants for the first month.

As always, using a lower quality soil is obviously an alternative and as long as you provide your plants with the proper nutrients, they will still grow into great plants. In the vegetative state, you'll need to give your plants nutrients that are high in nitrogen. There are many websites that offer full sets of the nutrients you'll need to feed your plants. Something to consider when finding which nutrients, you'll purchase is whether to use organic or chemical nutrients. Both have great attributes and neither is bad for your crop. The only difference is organic is not recommended for hydroponics while chemical is the *only* alternative for that process. Since we are only covering the tent or room method, we don't need to worry about hydro.

Organic nutrients provide a better smell and taste to your buds. Additionally, this is a more natural route to take meaning the nutrients provided in organic mixtures are closer to what your plants would be getting if they grew out in the wild. Chemical nutrients will give your buds increased potency and they will grow faster. What it comes down to with nutrients is preference. If smell and taste are more important, go with organic. If potent and slightly faster harvests are what you're looking for, purchase chemical. It really is that simple.

Finally, let's talk briefly about clones as this is the point from which we will begin and then go through the other stages of growing cannabis. In its simplest definition, a clone is a branch taken from a mother (remember that plants producing buds you can smoke will **always** be female), and placed in a pot to grow. What's great about clones is the toughest part of growing has already been done. Don't get me wrong. This process isn't simple. However, not having to start from seedlings saves a lot of time and effort.

Chapter Two-The Tent

Since this is a basic guide to growing marijuana, we are going to detail the simplest route to get your crop going. As previously discussed, there are various sizes of tents and boxes you can purchase to grow cannabis. The tent pictured below was purchased on Amazon. Before deciding which brand to buy, read the reviews. It'll be tempting to get a cheaper tent or box, but as mentioned earlier, you'll need to spend money up front to reap the rewards of not having to purchase cannabis in the future. It'll be worth it.

Tent: Side view

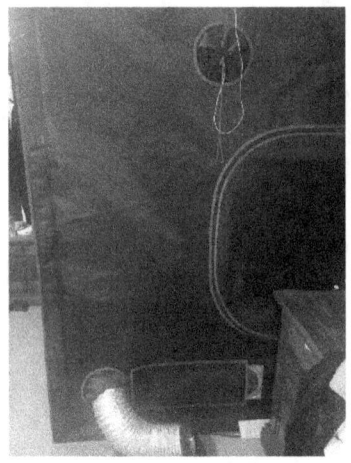

Tent: Inside view with plants

Before we delve into the details of the tent, this is a good place to mention not overdoing it on your first grow. As you can see, there are eight plants in the picture. Not only did it take a tremendous amount of time to tend to these plants during vegetation and flowering, harvest was a sixteen-hour process. That didn't include hanging the buds to dry, which was another three hours. Although this is an exciting new endeavor, start out with a little less ambition so as to not overwhelm yourself when it comes time to harvest.

Moving on. After you've received your tent or box and it's been assembled, you'll need to make sure there is plenty of ventilation and circulating air for the plants. There should be a fan inside the tent blowing on the crop during the vegetative state. This helps keep it cool during the sixteen to eighteen hours of light they will require, as well as helps the plants grow strong.

Pictured above, you'll see what appears to be foil lining the tent. The reflective interior optimizes the light that surrounds the plants. If you've purchased a tent that doesn't have the mylar (reflective interior), you'll want to line your tent with that. To get maximum efficiency, you'll need between ninety-two and ninety-four percent mylar or reflection.

Previously, we talked about fans for the tent and how important it is to have them blowing at all times so that the plants grow sturdy branches. In a tent that is reflective, you'll need to use *white* fans. White will reflect the most light. If you were unable to purchase mylar or a reflective tent or box, paint everything white. All equipment and lining will need to be white, which is the next best thing to the reflective material pictured above.

On a side note, there is one thing in your tent that should never be white or reflective and that is your pots. The roots of the plant are deeply implanted into the soil and should not be exposed to light. Doing so will harm or kill your crop at which point you would need to begin the process once again.

Since the tent will not come with everything you need, you'll want to purchase a hood. This is where the light will hang from and point down on your plants. As we've said a few times now, the upfront cost is a bit intimidating. Making a list of everything you'll need and purchasing items one or two at a time will help.

If smell is something you're trying to conceal, it is recommended to get a carbon filter. This piece of equipment's sole purpose is to cover up the smell of those plants as they start to flower and grow potent buds.

You'll also need an indoor/outdoor thermometer. Digital works best as it also shows the humidity inside the tent. As the plants begin to grow and get closer to the flowering stage, you'll want to monitor both the humidity and the temperature closely. With the lights on, growth will occur in the range of seventy-four to seventy-nine degrees. If it hits eighty degrees, that is the danger zone and can kill the plants. Anything below seventy-four isn't necessarily concerning unless it is consistently low. The plant will take much longer to grow if the tent isn't kept at the optimum temperature, which is seventy-six. These particular plants love light, but not the heat.

Optimum humidity is approximately forty percent. As the plants grow, it can increase, but you don't want it to go above seventy percent. At that level, you risk molds and mildews, which will affect the plants. Should your crop get mildew, which looks like white blotches, it can be treated. However, mildew and mold are much like a virus that isn't ever completely cured. It will appear to go away, but will never truly be gone. The mildew can make its way onto the buds, at which point you would need to start over because smoking mildew or mold could be deadly.

Proper ventilation is key to ensuring good growth. You'll need a high output exhaust fan; one that is powerful enough to exhaust the room or tent within approximately two to four minutes. With the exhaust fan, you'll want to get a fan-speed controller. You won't always want to run your exhaust at full speed. While your crop is growing, the fan will run to keep good air flow through the tent. There will be minimal ventilation needed, unless you live in an area with high humidity. If so, you'll want to keep an eye on the humidity portion of your tents thermometer.

Finally, you'll need a ballast from 400 to 1000 watts. This should be adjustable to dim the lights during certain phases of growth.

Let's quickly recap the things you'll need for your tent. First and foremost, the tent with white or mylar reflective walls, high output exhaust fan, an oscillating fan for inside the tent for optimal plant strength, a smaller inlet fan, indoor/outdoor thermometer, LED or HID lights along with the housing or hood that have ports for ventilation, and a ballast. If cost is an issue, prioritize your list and as stated earlier, buy one or two items at a time until you've collected everything you'll need for a great, first grow.

Chapter Three-Vegetative Growth

This is the phase in which your plant will really start to grow. If you've taken care of the ladies properly up to this point, they've established strong roots. Since cannabis is an annual plant, it will remain in the vegetative state as long as you'd like, provided the light is on for at least eighteen hours per day. This is where you trick the plants into continuing to grow as tall as space permits. It is extremely important to remember to keep your plants trimmed in this stage. When it comes to harvest, it'll be far less work for you.

During the vegetative stage, your plants are under the lights discussed previously for *eighteen hours.* That's right. The cannabis is spending almost an entire day sunning themselves under the high powered light. Because they are bathed in light for so long, and they are growing quickly, plants need to be watered regularly during this phase. A good rule of thumb for watering is if you can stick your finger about three quarters of an inch into the soil and still feel moisture, watering that day is unnecessary. Be very careful with this method to avoid letting the soil get too dry and risk harming the plant.

Even though the plants are getting nice and tall, they are still susceptible to serious damage. Following a strict regimen of light, watering and giving the plants nutrients will ensure a successful crop. This phase is pretty easy as long as you maintain a proper regimen. It's good to prune the plant at this stage. If you let it get out of control, it'll look like the photo below. Again, if the plants get out of control, it makes for a much longer process during harvest. You'll also want to watch for dead or dying leaves. Cut those as soon as you spot them to keep your plants healthy and happy.

How to Grow Marijuana

Believe it or not, the photo above is only eight plants. During the first attempted grow, I did get too ambitious and while the end result was most definitely worth it, the time it took to pare the plants down and find all the buds during harvest was astronomical.

You'll water and use nutrients throughout the entire process. To avoid over or under watering, you could buy a water meter. This is not a necessity and they can be costly. The cheapest is around sixty dollars while the most expensive can reach three-hundred. Aside from the method we discussed previously, you can also lift the pot. If it is too light, the plant is too dry. If it is too heavy, you've given your plant too much water. This is a process that if followed correctly, you'll have no problem taking your crop through to harvest. While cannabis is not the toughest plant on the planet, it can be pretty resilient. Keep an eye on the ladies and they'll turn out just fine.

When you purchase your clones, they'll come in a small pot or even a solo cup. Obviously, that environment is not sustainable. As the plants grow, you'll need to transplant them into a larger pot. This can only be done during the vegetative phase. The best pots for transplanting will have holes in the bottom for water drainage. Depending on how long you keep your plants in the vegetative state, you'll transplant them up to three times. You'll know when your plant is ready for a new pot a couple of ways. First, if the roots are sticking out of the bottom, obviously it's time for a new pot. You can also do what is called *popping the plant*. Turn the plant upside down so that the stem goes through your fingers. Carefully pull the pot or solo cup away. If the roots are starting to peek through, it's safe to say you can repot the plant.

As a general rule of thumb, it'll be about seven to ten days after you've brought your plants home before they'll need a new pot. The bigger the pot, the less you'll have to water. However, it is not recommended that you go from a solo cup to the largest pot simply to avoid watering on a regular basis. Just know you'll need to repot your plants two to three times during the vegetative phase.

Keep an eye out on the leaves during this phase. Bright green leaves are a good sign that the transplant was successful.

Chapter Four- Flowering

Although cannabis plants will grow quite tall during the vegetative phase, they can nearly double in size while flowering. As buds start to appear, it will get wider and heavier. In the flowering stage, you'll be tricking the plant into thinking it needs to reproduce, or flower, before it dies. This is done by changing the amount of time they are under the lights. To do this, you'll simply keep a twelve and twelve schedule. Twelve hours of light and twelve hours of darkness. You won't see much in the way of flowering the first week. It'll take a little bit of time for those buds to start to appear. When they do, however, you'll want to pay close attention to the sex of the flowers. While you should have been given female clones at the shop, there is a possibility that a mistake was made and you received a male clone. The way to tell the difference is the male will have pollen sacks. A female clone will have tiny follicles that resemble hairs.

In addition to there being a mistake made at the grow shop, some plants can be hermaphroditic by nature. A hermaphrodite plant is one that can switch its sexual orientation from male to female or vice versa. Chemdog is famous for having this characteristic. It's a good idea to study up on strains to avoid those that have the hermaphrodite tendencies. Only a female plant will produce buds that have the THC component. Male plants are only for reproduction or hemp.

Now that we've covered those important issues, let's look at the flowering process and what you'll be doing during this phase of development. During the other stages, you can go into the tent at any time. In the flowering stage, you'll want to stay out of the tent while the lights are off. Any light that gets into the tent while it is dark can affect the photosynthesis. If you think you forgot to water and absolutely must check on your plants while it is dark, you can do so by using a green light. That is the only color that doesn't have any effect on the plant. All other lights surrounding your tent will need to be out. Additionally, consistently check for any pinholes in the tent that might allow light in during the flowering stage. For instance, if you have a cat and it likes to sharpen its claws on anything it sees, keep it away from the tent. Small holes can be repaired or covered, but larger ones might destroy the tent.

As we briefly mentioned, you won't see an immediate change in the plants once you've moved into the flowering stage. They are transitioning from vegetative growth to flowering. During the entire flowering process, you'll want to keep an eye on your plants to make sure they aren't showing those hermaphroditic tendencies we discussed. Pruning the bottom of the plants helps to keep it growing upward and it wards against those pesky hermaphrodites.

At the four week mark is where you'll see an increase in bud growth. This is where the plant can get very heavy and you'll want to keep a close eye on them. If they start to tip over, they can be tied up with bamboo sticks. This is done by placing the bamboo in the soil toward the center of the stem. The roots have expanded in the pots and you'll want to avoid damaging them with the bamboo. Garden twist ties are recommended for securing your plant to the bamboo. Using any other kind of thread or twine might introduce debris to the plants. Since bud is sticky, it can pull hair, lint or fibers onto it, affecting the efficacy of the bud once it's been harvested.

There are some easy steps to take in order to avoid bringing outside junk into the tent that could ultimately become stuck to the plant. Make sure your clothes are clean. If your hair is long, tie it back. Keep any and all pets away from the tent. Their fur would be impossible to remove from the plants. Never wear shoes that you've worn outside into the tent. The soles pick up a lot of bugs, hairs and fibers throughout the day and you'll want to keep all of those as far away from your plants as possible.

Flowering will take approximately eight to fourteen weeks depending on the strain you purchased. Indicas have a shorter flower time where sativas are longer. You'll know when your buds are ready to harvest when the hairs go from white to red. There are crystals on the bud that will go from clear or white to orange. You'll need a loop or magnifying glass to be able to clearly see the hairs and crystals.

Don't forget that mold, mildew and pests can appear at any time during your grow. Always inspect leaves and soil to make sure nothing harmful has shown up.

Chapter Five-Harvest

Congratulations! Your plants survived and have produced big, wonderfully smelling buds. Now, it's time to cut down the plants and get them ready for the final stage, drying, which we'll discuss in detail a little later.

First and foremost, you absolutely must stop using nutrients seven to ten days *before* harvest. Optimally, you'll want to only water for two full weeks before you start to harvest. If the nutrient process is not stopped, your buds will taste like the chemicals used during the process, which is obviously not at all ideal. You've waited this long to reap the rewards of growing your own plants. Don't cut corners and stop nutrients at least ten days prior to harvest.

After those ten days, consider leaving the plants in complete darkness for a full twenty-four hours. Some growers have said that doing so makes the buds more resinous and better tasting. This is not necessary, however, and is up to the individual grower.

If you were on a budget and weren't looking at spending additional money on tools to harvest faster, a good old pair of scissors will do the trick. Regardless of how you choose to harvest, it will be a time consuming process. Some of the machines you can purchase are an aardvark trimmer or a grass trimmer. Both have a small vacuum that collects the leaves or trim. Most people agree that the added expense of buying those items isn't worth the time you'll save. Those devices are less precise and the majority prefer to use scissors or pruning shears. Those are relatively inexpensive and you might even have a pair lying around the house. Before you start to cut the leaves, put on a pair of latex gloves. The buds are incredibly sticky and wearing gloves will save you a lot of frustration from constantly having to get up and wash them.

It is also optional to remove the larger leaves on the plants two or three days before cutting the stems and buds. Keeping the plants manicured will cut down on the amount of time you'll spend harvesting. Again, this is not a requirement, nor will it affect the potency of your buds. It is merely a suggestion to minimize the amount of time you'll spend sitting and

trimming on harvest day.

Pictured above is a plant that is ready to harvest. Notice all the leaves that surround the buds. Carefully trim the leaves making sure that the stem remains intact. This will be an important part of the drying process. Without the stem, there is no good way to hang the plant upside down.

Chapter Six-Drying

This is the final step required before being able to fully reap the rewards of your first crop, which is smoking those beautiful buds. The drying phase has some important facts to remember as well. The air and temperature inside the tent will need to be maintained to optimize drying. This is not a part of the process that can be rushed.

The temperature inside the tent will need to be kept between sixty-five and seventy-five degrees. Humidity should be between forty-five and fifty-five percent. There will be no light allowed in the tent. Please note that unlike the flowering stage, if you walk into the tent and the light outside is on, it will not kill the buds or adversely affect the taste or potency. Really, there isn't much reason to check on the buds during this phase and contact with them should be minimal. The drying process in drier climates will take four to five days. In higher humidity areas, it can take up to two weeks.

This is a difficult time for the buds. While you shouldn't handle the buds regularly, a good way to tell if it's ready to smoke is by its flexibility. If the bud easily snaps off the stem, it's ready. If it is still clinging to the stem, leave it another couple of days. In order to keep from constantly touching the buds to check on them, wait a few days before you start to check the flexibility. Again, if you are in a more humid climate, the drying process is going to take longer even if you are running your tent at the above mentioned temperature and humidity. Don't try to rush any part of the process along, but especially try to refrain at this stage. You've taken your crop this far and it would be a bummer to ruin it by becoming impatient.

Once the buds are ready to come off the stem, there is one final process called curing. This is a very broad step and there are many ways to cure the buds. I've found it to be an unnecessary step. However, I live in a state that is pretty dry and have no real reason to cure the buds. The use of mason jars for storage has worked perfectly. Keep an eye on the buds and make sure that no matter which storage method you use, they are not collecting moisture. Again, this tends to be an issue in southern states where humidity is high. If you live in such a state, look into curing methods to avoid water damage due to condensation from humidity.

Chapter Seven-Recap and Suggestions

Choosing your medium is the first step. As outlined in this book, we chose to detail growing in a tent. It is also one of the cheapest and most effective ways to grow a great crop. Remember, don't be too cheap when it comes to the materials you'll need. While the tent is a great and less expensive way to grow, that doesn't mean purchase a cheap tent without the proper reflective material inside.

Your plants need lots of light and just the right amount of water and nutrients. Make sure you are careful and control the temperature, humidity and air quality in the tent.

Growing is not a quick process. You can control the vegetative phase, but the longer the plant can grow, the better buds it'll produce in the end. Ultimately, this process requires a lot of time and patience. The end result makes it worth the wait.

Now that you've made it through an entire grow and produced awesome buds, it's time to enjoy them. I'd like to close with a few suggestions to make your first grow great.

1. Watch for any changes in the plants. Earlier in this book, we talked about mold, mildew and pests. Since this is a plant you will ultimately be smoking, the use of pesticides and other harsh chemicals is unacceptable and incredibly harmful. There are lots of resources online to guide you through the cleansing process should you encounter any of these issues during your grow.
2. As strange as it may sound, positive energy, music and even words spoken to your plants is great for them. Plants are living, breathing beings and respond to the environment around them. Playing classical music seems to have worked well for my plants. They've turned out great every time.
3. Always clean your utensils with rubbing alcohol. If for some reason one crop had an issue with mold or pests, you wouldn't want to transfer that to the next crop by being careless. Also make sure that the tent the plants are raised in is also clean. Don't walk into

How to Grow Marijuana

    it with the shoes you wore outside. You wouldn't want to inadvertently introduce something damaging from the outside environment to your plants.

4. There are many nutrients you can use for your crop. We discussed the difference between organic based and chemical based nutrients. Tiger Bloom is a great, organic based option and has worked well for my crop.
5. Some soils already have nutrients in them. Most will have two weeks where you won't need to add organic or chemical nutrients. Doing so could kill the plants early on.

Conclusion

Thank you again for downloading this book!

I hope this book was able to help you to understand the marijuana growing process and growing your first marijuana!

The next step is to go and enjoy them!

Finally, if you enjoyed this book, then I'd like to ask you for a favor, would you be kind enough to leave a review for this book? It'd be greatly appreciated!

Thank you and good luck!

www.ingramcontent.com/pod-product-compliance
Lightning Source LLC
Chambersburg PA
CBHW052107110526
44591CB00013B/2390